A BLUE BANNER BIOGRAPHY

# Ashlee Simpson

*Marylou Morano Kjelle*

P.O. Box 196
Hockessin, Delaware 19707
Visit us on the web: www.mitchelllane.com
Comments? email us: mitchelllane@mitchelllane.com

*Mitchell Lane*
**PUBLISHERS**

| Printing | 2 | 3 | 4 | 5 | 6 | 7 | 8 | 9 |
| --- | --- | --- | --- | --- | --- | --- | --- | --- |

## Blue Banner Biographies

| | | |
| --- | --- | --- |
| Alan Jackson | Alicia Keys | Allen Iverson |
| Ashanti | **Ashlee Simpson** | Ashton Kutcher |
| Avril Lavigne | Beyoncé | Bow Wow |
| Britney Spears | Christina Aguilera | Christopher Paul Curtis |
| Clay Aiken | Condoleezza Rice | Daniel Radcliffe |
| Derek Jeter | Eminem | Eve |
| 50-Cent | Gwen Stefani | Ice Cube |
| Jamie Foxx | Ja Rule | Jay-Z |
| Jennifer Lopez | J. K. Rowling | Jodie Foster |
| Justin Berfield | Kate Hudson | Kelly Clarkson |
| Kenny Chesney | Lance Armstrong | Lindsay Lohan |
| Mariah Carey | Mario | Mary-Kate and Ashley Olsen |
| Melissa Gilbert | Michael Jackson | Miguel Tejada |
| Missy Elliott | Nelly | Orlando Bloom |
| Paris Hilton | P. Diddy | Peyton Manning |
| Queen Latifah | Rita Williams-Garcia | Ritchie Valens |
| Ron Howard | Rudy Giuliani | Sally Field |
| Selena | Shirley Temple | Tim McGraw |
| Usher | | |

**Library of Congress Cataloging-in-Publication Data**
    Ashlee Simpson / by Marylou Morano Kjelle.
          p. cm. –– (A blue banner biography)
    Includes discography (p.  ), filmography (p.  ), bibliographical references (p.  ), and index.
    ISBN 1-58415-383-0 (library bound)
       1. Simpson, Ashlee—Juvenile literature. 2. Singers—United States—Biography—Juvenile literature. I. Title. II. Series.
    ML3930.S568K54 2005
    782. 42164'092—dc22
                                                         2005009682

ISBN-10: 1-58415-383-0                              ISBN-13: 978-1-58415-383-2

**ABOUT THE AUTHOR: Marylou Morano Kjelle** is a freelance writer who lives and works in central New Jersey. Marylou writes a column for the *Westfield Leader/Times of Scotch Plains — Fanwood* called "Children's Book Nook," where she reviews children's books. She has written fifteen nonfiction books for young readers and co-authored and edited others. Marylou has a M.S. degree in Science from Rutgers University and teaches both science and writing at a community college in New Jersey.

**PHOTO CREDITS:** Cover, p. 4 Frederick M. Brown/Getty Images; p. 12 Jon Kopaloff/Getty Images; p. 19 Kevin Mazur/WireImage; p. 22 Rick Diamond/WireImage; p. 26 John Barrett/Globe Photos; p. 28 Theo Wargo/WireImage

# CONTENTS

When she was a young girl, Ashlee would look at pictures of women on the covers of magazines and wish she could be them. Now it is she who is a cover girl. Ashlee loves to dress in what she calls a "random" way with items of clothing that don't always match. Here she is in one of her signature outfits.

# "A Bummer"

*T*he crowd clapped and cheered as *Saturday Night Live* host Jude Law introduced Ashlee Simpson and her band on October 24, 2004. It was Ashlee's second time on the stage that night. Earlier, Ashlee had wowed the audience with her hit single, "Pieces of Me." Now, as she was getting ready to sing "Autobiography," the musical introduction for "Pieces of Me" began to play again. As she realized it was the wrong song, Ashlee looked back at the band with a puzzled look on her face. Then she did a little dance and walked off the stage.

Ashlee at first blamed her band for the mishap. They played the wrong song, she explained. Later her father, Joe Simpson, who is also her manager, revealed that Ashlee had acid reflux disease. This is an irritation of the esophagus that is caused by acid in the stomach. The condition was making it hard for her to sing. She had planned to "lip-sync" (sing along with a recording) in order to give the audience a better performance. But her drummer cued in the wrong guided-vocal backing track. Instead of "Autobiography," "Pieces of Me" began to play again.

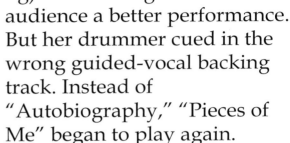

*The remarks were hurtful because many recording artists lip-sync, especially when they appear on television.*

"I was so sick and my voice doctor said I just couldn't sing live that night. [When] the wrong vocals came on, you can't imagine the state of shock I was in," Ashlee told *Teen People*.

The *Saturday Night Live* incident gave those who don't care for Ashlee's music a reason to further criticize her. They called her a fraud and said she had to resort to lip-synching because she has no talent. Ashlee even received hate mail on her website.

The harsh remarks upset Ashlee. They were particularly hurtful because many recording artists do lip-sync, especially when they appear on television.

"I write my own music! I sit in the studio for hours. That's my voice. It's a total slap in the face...The people who come to my concerts know the truth," she continued in her *Teen People* interview.

In the following weeks, video clips of Ashlee's *Saturday Night Live* performance were aired over and over again on all of the major news shows. They also appeared on the Internet. People ridiculed her and joked about her performance. But Ashlee wouldn't let herself be brought down by the experience. She continued to perform on stage, and also tape *The Ashlee Simpson Show*, her MTV reality television show. "All I can do is continue to work hard and do my best at the thing I love," she told *Cosmopolitan*.

**But Ashlee wouldn't let herself be brought down by the experience. She continued to perform on stage.**

It also helped that she could look at the situation humorously. A few nights after *Saturday Night Live*, Ashlee and her band were performing at the Radio Music Awards in Las Vegas. Ashlee stunned the audience by stopping her band in the middle of a song and scolding them for playing the wrong song. Then she flashed a bright smile at her audience. "Just kidding," she said, laughing at her own joke.

"It was a blip in her career, and it's incredible how she's bounced back. Most people would have curled up in a ball, but she faced it head-on," Jim Merlis, a representative of Ashlee's recording company, Geffen Records, explained to *Cosmopolitan*.

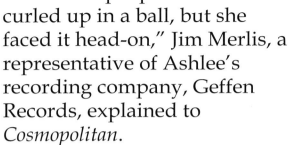

*But if one good thing has come from the mix-up, it is the amount of undying support she has received from her fans.*

Ashlee does not want to experience another performance like the one on *Saturday Night Live*. She has made changes in her life to help her acid reflux problem. She is taking medication for the disorder. She doesn't eat after 9:00 at night, and she has stopped eating dairy foods altogether. And she doesn't talk for one hour before a performance.

To Ashlee, the *Saturday Night Live* experience was "a bummer." But if one good thing has come from the mix-up, it is the amount of undying support she has received from her fans. "It's cool how the fans have been supportive," she said to *Cosmopolitan*. Knowing she is still a superstar in their eyes has helped her move on.

# Little Sister

**A**shlee Nicole Simpson was born on October 3, 1984 in Waco, Texas, to Tina and Joe Simpson and grew up in Dallas. Tina was an aerobics instructor and Joe was a Baptist youth minister and counselor. They met at church. Ashlee's sister, Jessica, a popular entertainer and one of the stars of the reality TV series, *Newlyweds: Nick & Jessica*, is four years older. Joe's position as a minister didn't pay much, and the family was constantly in debt. "When I was growing up, we didn't have any money at all and my dad had to work three jobs to take care of us," Ashlee told Zena Burns of *Teen People*.

With a father in the ministry, church was a big part of the Simpsons' family life. Ashlee, however, was restless in church. Once there, she would do all she could to draw attention away from her father and to herself. When she got older, Ashlee resented having to share her father with other young people in the congregation. "My dad was like a dad to a ton of other kids," she said in an interview with *The New York Times.*

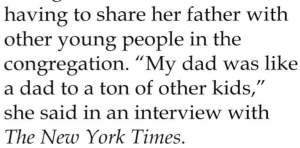

*Joe and Tina Simpson's focus on Jessica's career sometimes made Ashlee feel like an outcast.*

Ashlee began studying classical ballet when she was three years old. Beginning at age 11, she spent two summers without her family in New York City at the School of American Ballet. It was a great accomplishment for Ashlee, but it didn't stop her from living in the shade cast by her older sister's shadow. Jessica was an all-American sweetheart, a popular homecoming queen who sang solo in the church choir. By the time Jessica was a teenager, Joe and Tina Simpson knew she had the potential to make it big as a singer. Their focus on their oldest daughter's career sometimes made Ashlee feel like an outcast. She resorted to outrageous behavior, like playing the guitar naked, to get people to notice her. "I was dealing with my inner demons," Ashlee said in an interview with Virginia Heffernan of *The New York Times,* about how she struggled with feeling second best to Jessica, and unloved by her parents.

When she was thirteen, Ashlee was asked to dance with the Kirov Ballet in St. Petersburg, Russia. The Kirov is one of the most famous ballet companies in the world. Ashlee's father, who was Jessica's manager, said she couldn't go. Jessica's career was on the upswing, and he was relocating the family to Los Angeles.

Jessica knew how difficult it was for Ashlee to turn down the opportunity to dance in Russia. In 1999, she invited Ashlee to join her tour as a background dancer. Ashlee left school and studied between shows. "When everyone else got to play, I'd have to sit down and do work in the back of the bus," she told *The New York Times*. With the help of her mother, and other members of the

> *When she was thirteen, Ashlee was asked to dance with the Kirov Ballet in St. Petersburg, Russia.*

*Ashlee attends the premiere of* The Hot Chick *in Century City, California in December 2002. Those who follow Ashlee's career predict she will be just as successful a movie star as she is a musician. Joe Simpson, Ashlee's father and manager, currently advises her on what screen parts to accept, but he realizes that one day, Ashlee will be making those decisions herself. Ashlee's movie* Undiscovered *will be released in 2005.*

road crew who tutored her, Ashlee earned her high school diploma when she was sixteen.

Being part of Jessica's tour had highs and lows for Ashlee, who is very independent and likes to do things her own way. "My sister was this celebrity pop star and I…was so sick of everyone telling me you have to look like this, dance like this," said Ashlee to Janelle Brown of *Seventeen Magazine.* "I remember coming back [from the tour] and I was…ready to do my thing and be *me,*" she continued.

> *Not yet ready to break into the music business, Ashlee decided to try another aspect of entertainment: acting.*

Not yet ready to break into the music business, Ashlee decided to try another aspect of entertainment: acting. In 2000, she began auditioning for television and movie roles. The following year, she made an appearance in the Emmy-award winning sitcom, *Malcolm in the Middle*, starring Frankie Muniz. Then she had a small role as Monique in the movie comedy, *The Hot Chick*, which was released in 2002.

When Ashlee heard that WB's hit series, *7th Heaven* was looking to expand its cast of characters,

Ashlee auditioned for the part of Cecilia Smith, Simon's (David Gallagher) new girlfriend. After two successful seasons with the show, Ashlee felt it was time to move on. She knew that she could dance. She had proven that she could act. Now she was ready to focus on what she really wanted to do with her life: write, record, and perform her own music. Could she make it as a rock star? It was time to become a brunette, sign with a record company and find out.

> *Now she was ready to focus on what she really wanted to do with her life: write, record, and perform her own music.*

# Autobiography

Ashlee began preparing for a music career while she was still acting. Once taping was done for the day, she would sit in her trailer and write songs, or go to a recording studio to record them. At first Ashlee kept her decision to become a performer to herself. She didn't want to use Jessica's fame to further her own career. "I …thought that [singing] was Jessica's thing and that I was supposed to do something else," Ashlee said in an interview with *Girl's Life.*

However, Ashlee liked her own songs and she liked the music she was writing. Eventually, Ashlee realized that she could have a singing career in her own right, apart from Jessica. "I started writing my own music and decided I really liked my songs. [I realized] just because I have a sister who sings doesn't mean I can't be a singer too," she continued in her *Girl's Life* interview.

In 2003, Disney released *Freaky Friday*, a movie about a mother and her teenage daughter who change bodies after receiving Chinese fortune cookies. Ashlee's song, "Just Let Me Cry" appeared on the movie soundtrack. Ashlee has long admired female musicians like Chrissie Hynde, Joan Jett, Jewel, Joan Osborne, Stevie Nicks, Deborah Harry and Pat Benatar. "Just Let Me Cry" didn't have the rock sound Ashlee had grown up playing in her garage, but it got her music noticed. It also gave Ashlee the confidence to go out on a limb and create her own CD with her own lyrics.

*Ashlee's style, personality and music are the opposite of Jessica's. At first Ashlee had to fight being turned into a clone of her sister.*

Ashlee's style, personality and music are the opposite of Jessica's. At first Ashlee had to fight being turned into a clone of her sister. "There were definitely [recording] labels that turned me down because I wanted to do an indie kind of thing," Ashlee told *Cosmopolitan* magazine, when they named her their "Fun Fearless Female of the Year" for 2005. Ashlee's father, who is now her manager as well as Jessica's, found one record company willing to take a chance on an independent Ashlee. She signed a recording contract with Geffen Records. In the summer of 2004, her first single, "Pieces of Me," a song Ashlee wrote about her then-boyfriend, singer/songwriter Ryan Cabrera, was released.

Ashlee introduced "Pieces of Me" on MTV's *Total Request Live*. She was soon off and running on a tour that included radio stations and retail stores. It was important to both her father and Geffen Records executives that Ashlee be noticed by the public and recognized for who she was, not just for her music.

> *By September, 2004, Autobiography had gone triple platinum, meaning it had sold 3 million copies.*

On July 20, 2004, Ashlee's first CD, *Autobiography* was released. It sold 400,000 copies the week it was released. Within three weeks, *Autobiography* had sold nearly a million copies. By September 2004, the CD had gone triple platinum, meaning it had sold 3 million copies. "It's unheard of in this business—even for a superstar—to sell this number of records," Jordon Schur, Geffen Records co-president, told *Seventeen Magazine*. "No one in the world knew who she *was* four months ago." "Pieces of Me" and Ashlee went on to win two 2004 Teen Choice Awards – "Best Summer Song" and "Fresh Face."

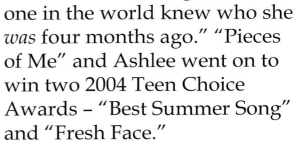

*One song, "Shadow," addresses how Ashlee felt about Jessica when they were growing up.*

Each recording on *Autobiography* expresses Ashlee's emotions about her personal experiences. "My inspiration came from what I have gone through in the past three years. Every single day I was thinking of what I was going through and would write songs about it," Ashlee told her fans in an MSN Live Online chat. One song, "Shadow," addresses how Ashlee felt about Jessica when they were growing up. "[The song is] about my sister and it's about finding my identity and finding who I am as a person and what it is that I'm gonna be and all that kind of stuff," Ashlee explained to Jennifer Vineyard in an MTV interview. "It's about coming into my own."

One of the reasons for *Autobiography's* success is that it contains open-hearted lyrics that young people everywhere can relate to. Ashlee sings of self-awareness obtained through love, heartbreak and sexual awakening. "I'm nineteen and I'm going through some defining moments of my life. I'm trying not to hold anything back," she told Chuck Taylor of *Billboard* Magazine in July 2004.

*Ashlee's childhood was filled with music, dancing and singing. She actually got started as a musician by playing with a band in her garage. Writing and singing songs is a means of self-expression for Ashlee. Here she is performing on stage.*

"Pieces of Me" and an accompanying video clip were posted on AOL. They received about one million hits per month for several months.

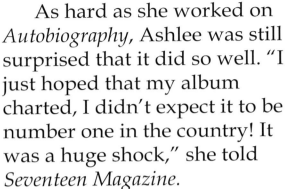

**Ashlee feels creating *Autobiography* was a therapeutic experience that has made her stronger.**

As hard as she worked on *Autobiography*, Ashlee was still surprised that it did so well. "I just hoped that my album charted, I didn't expect it to be number one in the country! It was a huge shock," she told *Seventeen Magazine*.

Ashlee feels creating *Autobiography* was a therapeutic experience that has made her stronger and helped her grow as a person. "Anything I had on my shoulders, I got to put out there. It enabled me to find out who I am, to discover my identity in the world," she said on her website, www.ashleesimpsonmusic.com

# Facing Reality

*O*n June 16, 2004, Ashlee's reality TV show, *The Ashlee Simpson Show*, premiered on MTV. More than two and a half million viewers tuned in to watch. The show was the brainchild of Joe Simpson, who had developed a similar show for Jessica called *Newlyweds: Nick and Jessica*. As a result of *Newlyweds*, Jessica's public image, as well as her record sales, had skyrocketed. With *Autobiography* about to be released, Ashlee's father knew that a reality show of her own would give the viewing public a chance to get to know her, apart from Jessica. The plan was for a camera crew to follow Ashlee 24 hours a day, as they captured the drama of her life on tape. Each episode focused on one song from *Autobiography*: why it was written and how it was recorded.

At first, Ashlee had been against the idea of a reality show. She'd been a part of *Newlyweds: Nick and Jessica* and knew what it was like to be surrounded by cameras all the time. Her father, however, finally won her over. Ashlee told *Cosmopolitan* that her dad said, "It's going to be good for you because people need to see your personality and see that you're not the same person

*Ashlee with her parents, Tina (left) and Joe Simpson. The Simpson family is closely-knit; and Ashlee often turns to her parents, as well as to older sister, Jessica, for emotional support.*

as Jessica. They need to see how you make your record, and that you're doing it yourself."

Having played a character (Cecilia Smith on *7th Heaven*) and acted as herself on *The Ashlee Simpson Show*, Ashlee is sometimes asked the difference between acting in both roles. Despite the lack of privacy, Ashlee thinks it's easier to play herself. As she told Cosmopolitan, "[*The Ashlee Simpson Show*] showed me very close to who I am. I have a few different sides. I'm goofy but at the same time, I'm tough and at the same time I am sensitive and nice."

Ashlee feels that having her own show allows her fans to get to know her personally, and to see that she is an everyday person that they can relate to. *The Ashlee Simpson Show* also helped differentiate the two Simpson sisters once and for all. "People expected me to be just like Jessica. So, I thought [the show] was the smartest way to put an end to the comparisons," Ashlee told *Seventeen Magazine*.

Within a month of debuting, *The Ashlee Simpson Show* was the one of the highest rated shows on

> **Within a month of debuting, The Ashlee Simpson Show was the one of the highest rated shows on cable TV.**

cable TV. Week after week, Ashlee's fans tuned in to watch both the highs and lows of her life. They saw her morph into a multi-platinum recording artist while dealing at the same time with the breakup of her relationship with singer Josh Henderson. Fans also had glimpses of how Ashlee deals with her stardom, including preparations for her first nationwide tour.

*"The show was a success because Ashlee came across as a real person and not as a glamorous star," said Brian Graden.*

"The show was a success because Ashlee came across as a real person and not as a glamorous star," said Brian Graden, president of entertainment for MTV Network's Music Group, to *Television Week. The Ashlee Simpson Show* allowed Ashlee's fans to see her as an every-day person they can relate to. The show also helped *Autobiography* reach multi-platinum levels.

The fans who watched *The Ashlee Simpson Show*, as well as purchased the CD, really felt as though they knew Ashlee. These two things together contributed to her success.

# Looking Ahead

*I*t wasn't easy growing up with a talented and beautiful older sister, but the hard feelings that Ashlee occasionally harbored towards Jessica are a thing of the past. Today the Simpson sisters are as close as ever. Although they differ in personal style (Jessica is glamorous and Ashlee is funky) and the types of music they perform (Jessica is a pop star and Ashlee is a rock star), the sisters are very supportive of one another's claims to fame.

Because their roads to stardom took opposite courses—Jessica was a recording artist before she starred in *Newlyweds: Nick and Jessica* and Ashlee was an actor in *7th Heaven* before becoming a recording artist—the sisters are able to advise one another on their careers. There is neither jealousy

Jessica and Ashlee are both talented performers, and each shares in the other's success. Although Jessica has been a role model for her younger sister, it is important to Ashlee that she retains her individuality.

nor competition between them, and they openly admit to being proud of each other's accomplishments.

Now that Ashlee has proven herself, she no longer has a need to distance herself from Jessica. People often ask her if Jessica Simpson is her sister. Of course, Ashlee says yes; then she tells the person that *she* is Jessica's sister, *too*. One of the highest compliments Ashlee feels she can receive is being compared to Jessica.

> **Now that Ashlee has proven herself, she no longer has a need to distance herself from Jessica.**

Despite being in show business, the Simpsons are a very close family. Ashlee's parents are proud of all that she has accomplished at such a young age. "We saw our children's talents and we were supportive of those talents," Ashlee's mother, Tina, told Jeff Leeds of *The New York Times*. "We have worked alongside with our kids. It's been like a family effort."

With a hit reality TV show and a multi-platinum record album behind her, Ashlee has every reason to look toward the future. She'd like to do more acting, and stars in the movie, *Undiscovered*. In the film, she plays a tomboy actress whose music helps her deal with life. However, Ashlee sees singing and performing as an important part of her life when she looks ahead. "I've wanted to do this forever!" Ashlee told *Teen People*. "I grew up performing. I have an out-there personality."

Ashlee recently purchased her parents' house in Studio City, California, where she lives with three girlfriends. Someday she'd like to move back to

*At one time Ashlee was so insecure about her singing that she would wait until she was alone in the house before she would belt out a tune. Now when she tours, she sings not only her own songs, but those of performers who made it big in the 1980's. Here Ashlee and her band clown around at an autograph event for "Autobiography" at the Virgin Megastore in Times Square NYC in 2004.*

Texas and own a ranch near Austin, with a built-in recording studio. Another of Ashlee's goals is to design her own line of clothing.

Ashlee has been linked romantically with several men in addition to Ryan Cabrera and Josh Henderson. While the demands of her career make it tough to stay in a relationship, eventually she would like to marry.

Despite a busy touring, singing and acting schedule, Ashlee still finds time to volunteer and help others. She worked with *Teen People* magazine to create an auction to benefit UNICEF'S relief efforts for the victims of the 2004 tsunami in south Asia.

*Despite a busy touring, singing and acting schedule, Ashlee still finds time to volunteer and help others.*

Ashlee's life is not all work and no play. When she does have a day off, she enjoys sitting in front of the television with a bowl of popcorn and watching movies. She also likes to bowl, cook, knit and shop for vintage clothing.

Ashlee can look ahead to a long career of many possibilities stretching in front of her. If her past is any indication, it will be a successful future indeed.

# CHRONOLOGY

**1984**  Born on October 3 in Waco, Texas
**1996**  Accepted by American School of Ballet in New York City
**1999**  Begins traveling with Jessica as a dancer
**2001**  Appears in guest role on *Malcolm in the Middle*
**2002**  Lands the role of Cecilia Smith in *7th Heaven*
**2002**  Plays Monique in movie, *The Hot Chick*
**2003**  *Freaky Friday* soundtrack is released with Ashlee's song, "Just Let Me Cry"
**2004**  *The Ashlee Simpson Show* debuts on June 16
**2004**  *Autobiography* is released on July 20
**2004**  Wins *Billboard* Music Award's New Female Artist of the Year; receives two awards in Nickelodeon's Teens' Choice Awards; appears on cover of *Seventeen* magazine
**2005**  Selected as *Cosmopolitan* magazine's Fun Fearless Female of the Year; stars in the movie, *Undiscovered*

# DISCOGRAPHY

CDs
**2004**    *Autobiography*

Singles
**2003**    "Just Let Me Cry"
**2004**    "Pieces of Me"
**2004**    "Shadow"
**2005**    "La La"

**2002** *The Hot Chick*
**2005** *Undiscovered*

## Books

Norwich, Grace. *Ashlee Simpson: Out of the Shadow and Into the Spotlight.*
New York: Simon and Schuster, 2005.

## Websites

Ashlee Simpson Official Website
http://www.ashleesimpsonmusic.com

Ashlee Simpson Fansite
http://www.ashleesimpson.net

Taylor, Chuck. "Singing's Not an Act for Ashlee Simpson."
http://www.entertainment-news.org/breaking/411/singings-
not-an-act-for-ashlee-simpson.html

Ashlee Simpson
http://www.answers.com/topic/ashlee-simpson

Hall, Sarah. "Ashlee Simpson Sings! (Really)," E! Online News
http://www.eonline.com/News/Items/0,1,15219,00.html

Ashlee Simpson
http://en.wikipedia.org/wiki/Ashlee_Simpson

Ashlee Simpson – Stories – E! Online
http://www.fanpages.com/Facts/People/Stories/
0,127,72570,00.html?celfact3

Vineyard, Jennifer. "The Rock Sister."
http://www.mtv.com/bands/s/simpson_ashlee/
news_feature_070604/

# INDEX